RAPTURE
IS IT WRITTEN?

LANE & SHARI RAMSEY
Written Word Publishing
Tulsa, Oklahoma

RAPTURE: IS IT WRITTEN?

Written Word Publishing
P.O. Box 54070
Tulsa, OK 74155

Table of Contents

Chapter Four (Continued)

Chapter Five - Study in Revelation 47

Chapter Six - Who Is Leaving First 63

Chapter Seven - God's Protection 71

Chapter Eight - New Beginnings 83

Scripture Index 91

Introduction

Recently, as we were involved in a study of end-time prophecy and how or if current events relate to prophecy, we came to realize what we had been taught and what we had always heard concerning the rapture seemed to be in contradiction to what God's Word says, or does not say, about it. This got us involved in a study of the rapture.

We had always heard that the rapture would take place prior to the tribulation and therefore Christians would not be going through the tribulation. This is commonly referred to as a pre-tribulation rapture.

There are some Christians who believe in a mid-tribulation rapture and others who believe in a post-tribulation rapture, meaning that Christians would experience all or part of the tribulation.

It never occurred to us previously to question what we had always heard about the rapture as this had come from pastors and teachers, whom one would assume being in their position, would know to what they were referring.

As we studied the Scriptures that are referenced in regard to the pre-tribulation belief, we began to have some questions regarding the interpretation of these verses. There were also questions regarding interpretation of Scripture relating to end-time prophecy, and how or if this prophecy would affect Christians. Obviously, if the rapture occurs before the tribulation, the events that will transpire throughout the tribulation will not affect Christians at all.

The question that needed answering then was, if there really is a rapture, whether it will take place before, during or after the tribulation.

We have heard it said, "It really doesn't matter if one Christian believes in a pre-tribulation rapture while another believes in a mid or post-tribulation rapture, let's all just get along and love each other in Christ."

Yes, we should love each other as the Lord has commanded. We should love each other enough to address the consequences and the seriousness of wrong teaching regarding this matter, and not allow people to continue in a gray area.

Too often we find ourselves accepting things simply because "that's what we've always heard" or "that's the way we've always done it". The purpose of this book is to see if "what we've always heard" aligns with what God's Word says, for ultimately, the Word of God is the only Word that matters.

We would only hope that as you read this book you will ask God to give you an open mind, not influenced by the traditions of men or by "what we've always heard". If it turns out that "what we've always heard" aligns with God's Word, fantastic, but if it does not, let go of it, get into God's Word, read and study it for yourself and learn the Truth.

Chapter One

RAPTURE

What is the Rapture? Although the word rapture is not in God's Word, some Christians use it to describe the catching up in the clouds to meet the Lord in the air that Paul talked about in I Thessalonians 4:17. It seems that no one questions the use of the word rapture to describe this "catching up", but rather, the question is: "When does the rapture take place?"

Different Viewpoints: Pre - Mid - Post

There are three main, different, viewpoints regarding the timing of the rapture. They are all centered around the tribulation, and are as follows:

Pre-Tribulation - meaning the rapture will occur before the tribulation, Mid-Tribulation - meaning the rapture will occur sometime during the tribulation, and Post-Tribulation - meaning the rapture will occur at the end of the tribulation. Throughout this book we will be using these terms in abbreviated form (pre-trib, mid-trib, and post-trib).

The pre-trib and mid-trib beliefs maintain the rapture will occur at some point in time before or during the seven year period of tribulation. Christ will appear in the air, the Christians will be caught up to meet Him, and then Christ will carry them off to Heaven so they will not have to go through the tribulation, or at least will only have to go through part of it.

The post-trib belief maintains the rapture will not take place until after the tribulation, meaning then that Christians will go through the tribulation.

What is the Purpose of the Rapture?

The rapture, when spoken of by pre-trib or mid-trib believers, means to be carried off to Heaven, with the purpose being for Christians not to have to endure all or part of the tribulation. Are we to assume then, that the rapture, as spoken of by post-trib believers, has the same meaning?

Obviously, the purpose could not be the same since the result of a post-trib rapture would be that Christians will go through the tribulation. But, does it mean that Christians will be caught up to meet the

Lord in the air and be carried off to Heaven as the pre-trib and mid-trib beliefs maintain?

If it does, then the question that might be relevant regarding a post-trib rapture is this: "What's the point?" At the end of the tribulation Christ returns to earth to set up His kingdom for one thousand years. Why would we be raptured then?

The Second Coming (In Part)

If the Lord comes before the tribulation to rapture Christians off to Heaven, then He comes again after the tribulation to set up His kingdom, does this mean the Second Coming of the Lord is divided into two parts?

Also, the pre-trib belief maintains there will be other people (from the ones left on earth that missed the rapture) that become Christians during the tribulation. If the first part of the Second Coming of the Lord is Christians being raptured before the tribulation, and the second part of the Second Coming of the Lord is when He returns to set up His kingdom on earth, what happens to the people who become Christians through the tribulation? Do they miss out on being raptured? Maybe there is a third part of the Second Coming. Are we confused yet?

"The Missing" Mystery

The pre-trib belief maintains the rapture is a secret. A secret, that is, to the non-Christians. When the Lord appears in the air to rapture Christians, only

Christians can see Him. The people left on earth will be scurrying around looking for their lost loved ones, totally oblivious to the fact the rapture has occurred or that there was even a rapture to occur.

Among the missing will be not only their loved ones that were alive when the rapture occurred, but also the graves will be opened up and their loved ones who have already died will be missing as well. Question: Is it Scriptural?

Another point of the pre-trib belief is that in the Book of Revelation the Church is mentioned throughout Chapters 1-3 and, they say, is not mentioned again after that, except in Revelation 4:1 where (the pre-trib belief maintains) the rapture takes place with the "Come up here".

The point being, the omission of the mention of the Church after Chapter 3 must mean the Church is not on earth through the tribulation, that is why it is not mentioned. When we get to our study in Revelation we will see if we can find out whether or not the Church is mentioned after Chapter 3.

What Difference Does It Make?

Some might ask, "What difference does it make which way a person believes?" First, the difference it makes is this; the people who believe in a pre-trib or mid-trib rapture are expecting Christ to come first (before the anti-christ) to rapture them away. In fact, we have heard it taught that Christians will not even know who the anti-christ is because they will have been raptured before he appears on the scene.

If, on the other hand, the rapture occurs at the end of the tribulation, at the time of the Lord's Second Coming, and the anti-christ appears before the Second Coming of the real Christ, they could be deceived into believing this false "Christ" is Christ since they are expecting Christ to appear to them (Christians) first to rapture them away. They could be deceived into following the wrong "Christ".

Second, if people believe they are going to go through the tribulation, this belief could influence their decisions in such areas as where to work, where to live, financial matters and what preparations need to be made to go through it. The people who believe they are going to be raptured out before the tribulation would of course have no need to concern themselves with making any preparations or decisions regarding living through it.

And third, if people believe the Lord is going to rapture Christians out before the tribulation (obviously the Lord loves the end-time group of Christians more than He has loved any other group of Christians throughout history, since some of them had to suffer through trials and tribulations and were not raptured) and they realize one day the time when the rapture should have occurred, as they had always been taught, has since come and gone, and here they are still on earth, this would not do too much in the way of strengthening their faith.

These are just a few of the reasons why we need to address the issue of different teachings concerning the rapture and when it will take place.

False Teaching?

How did these different teachings come about? Were they all derived from the Word of God? If God's Word teaches us of a pre-trib rapture how can it at the same time teach us of a post-trib rapture? Should we even use the word rapture since it is not in God's Word?

Inasmuch as I Corinthians 14:33 tells us that God is not the author of confusion, we would have to conclude that the confusion surrounding this subject is the result of false teachings, these false teachings becoming tradition; handed down from generation to generation. Instead of studying God's Word for ourselves we believe the tradition because "that's what we have always heard."

After reading and studying the Scriptures describing the end-times and the events that must take place before our Lord returns, it is not hard to understand why some Christians would find comfort in the belief that they will not be on earth during that time. However, the question is: Is it Scriptural? Let's turn to God's Word and eliminate the confusion.

Chapter Two

STUDY IN MATTHEW

W e will begin our study in the Book of Matthew, Chapter 24, and see what Jesus had to say concerning the end-time signs and events that must take place before He returns. Matthew 24:

3: **Now, as He was sitting on the Mount of Olives, the disciples came to Him privately, saying, "Tell us, when will these things be? And what will be the sign of your coming, and of the end of the age?"**

Jesus is sitting on the Mount of Olives talking to His disciples; His followers. The disciples, in their

second question, tie together Jesus' coming again to the
end of this age. Jesus is about to explain to them the
signs that will lead up to the end of this age and to His
Second Coming. This must mean that followers of
Jesus, Christians, will be on earth to recognize the
signs as they are happening.

The Beginning of Sorrows

**4:   And Jesus answered and said to them, "Take
         heed that no one deceives you."**
**5:   "For many will come in my name, saying, 'I
         am the Christ' and will deceive many."**

Christ - anointed, i.e., Messiah
Messiah - Usually a consecrated person (as a king,
          priest, or saint).
Consecrated - to set apart for a holy use, to represent as
          holy.

Jesus warned His followers to be careful not to
be deceived by someone coming, claiming to be
"Christ," or claiming to be anointed of God,
representing himself as holy or speaking words that he
claims to be from God. The fact that Jesus warned His
followers to be careful so they are not deceived means
if they are not careful there is a possibility they could
be deceived.

Jesus tells us there will be many who will come
in His name. These will lead to the arrival of the
ultimate deceiver; Satan.

6:      "And you will hear of wars and rumors of
        wars. See that you are not troubled; for all
        these things must come to pass, but the end is
        not yet."
7:      "For nation will rise against nation and
        kingdom against kingdom. And there will be
        famines, pestilences, and earthquakes in
        various places."
8:      "All these things are the beginning of
        sorrows."

There have always been wars, famines and
earthquakes, though they have continued to become
more numerous and more severe in the last century.

The word "sorrows" in Verse 8 means a pang or
throe, especially of child birth. Just as labor pains start
out mildly with several minutes in between, then
continue to come more quickly and more severe until
the birth, so also will the wars, famines, pestilences and
earthquakes come more quickly and more severe.

Just as a woman suffers labor pains when a new
life is about to be brought forth, so also will this world
suffer these pains as a new age is about to be brought
forth; when Christ sets foot on this earth and reigns as
King of kings and Lord of lords.

9:      "Then they will deliver you up to tribulation
        and kill you, and you will be hated by all
        nations for My name's sake."
10:     "And then many will be offended, will
        betray one another, and will hate one
        another."

The Book of Mark, Chapter 13, gives a more detailed account of this. In Mark, just as in Matthew, Jesus is talking to His disciples. We will look at the New Century Version. Mark 13:

9:   **"You must be careful. People will arrest you and take you to court and beat you in their synagogues. You will be forced to stand before kings and governors, to tell them about me. This will happen to you because you follow me."**

11:   **"When you are arrested and judged, don't worry ahead of time about what you should say. Say whatever is given you to say at that time, because it will not really be you speaking; it will be the Holy Spirit."**

12:   **"Brothers will give their own brothers to be killed, and fathers will give their own children to be killed. Children will fight against their own parents and cause them to be put to death."**

13:   **"All people will hate you because you follow me, but those people who keep their faith until the end will be saved."**

We see very clearly that it is Jesus' followers who are delivered up. Christians will be hated because they follow Jesus. They will be betrayed and caused to be delivered up. When they are delivered up they will be a witness for Christ as the Holy Spirit speaks through them. Matthew 24:

11:   **"Then many false prophets will rise up and deceive many."**

Unfortunately, many of these false prophets, who will be declaring false doctrine, will be standing in church pulpits. In Revelation 2:2 in Jesus' letter to the church of Ephesus He says, *"I know your works, your labor, your patience, and that you cannot bear those who are evil. And you have tested those who say they are apostles and are not, and have found them liars."*

We have to test what we hear to determine whether it is God's Word or the words of false teachers. How do we do this? 2 Timothy 2:15 tells us, *"Be diligent to present yourself approved to God, a worker who does not have to be ashamed, rightly dividing the word of Truth."*

We cannot rightly divide the word of truth if we do not know what the word of truth is. The King James Version says, *"Study to show thyself approved unto God..."* We need to study God's Word so we will know the truth and not be deceived.

Unfortunately though, as Verse 11 says, many will be deceived. Many false prophets will come teaching false doctrine. This will lead many people to be deceived; believing that the false "Christ" is really Christ.

The people who are deceived will be somebody's parents, children, brothers and sisters. They will betray you unknowingly because they will be deceived into believeing they are following Christ and want you to do the same. This is when Christians will be arrested and stand before kings and governors as a witness for Jesus, the Christ.

12:   "And because lawlessness will abound, the love of many will grow cold."

LAWLESSNESS ABOUNDS, MANY HAVE GROWN COLD! There are probably few among us who would be surprised to pick up their Sunday morning paper and see this as a headline.

13:   "But he who endures to the end shall be saved."

The New Century Version says, *"But those people who keep their faith until the end will be saved."* Who are the people who have the faith? Christians. Jesus says if we keep our faith TO THE END we will be saved. What does He mean "to the end"? If we go back and look at Verse 3, the question Jesus is answering is, "What will be the sign of Your coming, and of the END OF THE AGE?"

This must mean Christians will be here until the end of this age, and if we keep our faith until then we will be saved. Jesus did not say if we endure or keep our faith until the rapture we would be saved, He said, "to the end;" the end of this age.

14:   "And this Gospel of the kingdom will be preached in all the world as a witness to all the nations, and then the end will come."

The end will not come until the Gospel has been preached to every nation. Who is it that will preach the Gospel to every nation? Jesus is talking to His disciples (His followers) in Matthew 28:

19:   **"Go therefore and make disciples of all the nations, baptizing them in the name of the Father and of the Son and of the Holy Spirit,"**

20:   **"teaching them to observe all things that I have commanded you; and lo, I am with you always, even to the end of the age."**

Jesus' followers are to spread the Gospel to all the nations and they are to do so until the end of the age, not until the rapture.

In all of the above verses Jesus gives us many signs (and warnings) of things that must take place BEFORE He returns and before this present age ends. Why would Jesus spend His time giving His followers signs and warnings of things that would happen during the end-times if they were not going to be here to recognize them?

Great Tribulation

15:   **"Therefore when you see the 'abomination of desolation,' spoken of by Daniel the prophet, standing in the holy place, (whoever reads, let him understand),"**

16:   **"then let those who are in Judea flee to the mountains."**

17:    "Let him who is on the housetop not go down
       to take anything out of his house."
18:    "And let him who is in the field not go back
       to get his clothes."
19:    "But woe to those who are pregnant and to
       those who are nursing babies in those days!"
20:    "And pray that your flight may not be in
       winter or on the Sabbath."
21:    "For then there will be great tribulation,
       such as has not been since the beginning of
       the world until this time, no, nor ever shall
       be."
22:    "And unless those days were shortened, no
       flesh would be saved; but for the elect's sake
       those days will be shortened."

Jesus tells us that when we see the abomination of desolation standing in the holy place, then there will be a time of great tribulation. The days of the great tribulation will be shortened for the sake of the elect.

Who are the elect? In Colossians 3:12 Paul refers to believers as the "elect of God". So we see that the elect (Christians) will be here through the tribulation.

23:    "Then if anyone says to you, 'Look, here is
       the Christ!' or 'There!' do not believe it."
24:    "For false christs and false prophets will rise
       and show great signs and wonders to deceive,
       if possible, even the elect."
25:    "See, I have told you beforehand."

The false "Christ" will come before Christ and people will think he is really Christ. How could they be deceived like that? If they are taught and believe that Jesus is coming FIRST to rapture them out, when they see the false "Christ" arrive first, performing great wonders and miracles they will be deceived into believing it is Christ.

Revelation 13:13-14a tells us, *"He performs great signs, so that he even makes fire come down from heaven on the earth in the sight of men. And he deceives those who dwell on the earth by those signs which he was granted to do in the sight of the beast."*

This false "Christ" will fool even the elect if possible. How could that be possible? Because they do not know which "Christ" comes first. They have listened to words of false teachers instead of studying God's Word.

We want to note here that just in the few verses we have studied so far, Jesus has warned us four times (Verses 4,5,11 and 24) that we need to be careful not to be deceived. Why? Because we are going to be here and we need to know which "Christ" we are following.

We need to know which "Christ" comes first; the false "Christ". Jesus did not say that He is coming first to rapture Christians, but rather that the Christians who endure to the end, the end of this age, will be saved.

26:    **"Therefore if they say to you, 'Look, He is in the desert!' do not go out; or 'Look, He is in the inner rooms!' do not believe it."**

27:    **"For as the lightning comes from the east and flashes to the west, so also will the coming of the Son of Man be."**

28:    **"For wherever the carcass is, there the eagles will be gathered together."**

We are being warned by Jesus again not to follow the wrong "Christ". Even though the false "Christ" will deceive many by working great miracles you will not be deceived as long as you realize that the false "Christ" is coming before the real Christ.

When the real Christ returns no one will have to tell you where He is because EVERYONE will see Him. Jesus does not say He is coming back twice, the first time for just Christians to see and be raptured and the second time for everyone else to see.

Christ Returns

29:    **"Immediately after the tribulation of those days the sun will be darkened, and the moon will not give it's light; the stars will fall from heaven, and the powers of the heavens will be shaken."**

30:    **"Then the sign of the Son of Man will appear in heaven, and then all the tribes of the earth will mourn, and they will see the Son of Man coming on the clouds of heaven with power and great glory."**

31:    **"And He will send His angels with a great sound of a trumpet, and they will gather together His elect from the four winds, from one end of heaven to the other."**

The sign of the Son of Man will appear in heaven AFTER the tribulation, not before. All the tribes, everyone, on earth will see Him coming on the clouds. This does not sound as if it is a secret since everyone will see.

He will send His angels with a great sound of a trumpet. In I Corinthians 15:52a Paul tells us about Jesus' Second Coming, he says, *"In a moment, in the twinkling of an eye, at the last trumpet."* This shows us that the trumpet referred to in Verse 31 above is the last trumpet.

We all know what "last" means, there are no more. Jesus' Second Coming is the LAST act in the sequence of events that ends this age and begins the new one; His one thousand year reign on earth as King of kings and Lord of lords.

Again, we read of what happens at the last (seventh) trumpet in Revelation 11:

15:   Then the seventh angel sounded: And there were loud voices in heaven, saying, "The kingdoms of this world have become the kingdoms of our Lord and of His Christ, and He shall reign forever and ever!"

The seventh trumpet sounds and Christ returns to reign. Then He sends His angels to gather the elect from one end of Heaven to the other. The elect ARE NOT GATHERED until after all of the events occur that He has warned us about.

We will not be gathered until Christ returns. Christ returns after the tribulation with the sound of a trumpet, the last trumpet, then we are gathered together.

Know the Season

32:    "Now learn this parable from the fig tree:
       When it's branch has already become
       tender, and puts forth leaves, you know that
       summer is near."

33:    "So you also, when you see all these things,
       know that it is near - at the doors!"

34:    "Assuredly, I say to you, this generation will
       by no means pass away till all these things
       take place."

35:    "Heaven and earth will pass away, but My
       words will by no means pass away."

36:    "But of that day and hour no one knows, not
       even the angels of Heaven, but My Father
       only."

Jesus draws this parallel to show us that we can and should know the season in which we live. Although our Father is the only One who knows the exact day when Christ will return, we can and should know the season from the signs Jesus has given us. Just as we know when a tree begins to put forth leaves that it is spring, we also know summer is near. He has given us the signs to watch for so we will know when His return is near.

Verse 34 tells us the generation that sees these things (the signs that Jesus gave leading up to the end of this age) begin to take place, will not pass away before our Lord's Second Coming.

Verse 36 tells us the exact hour of Christ's return will not be known to anyone, except our Father, therefore being a surprise at least in the sense we will not know the exact hour, just the season. Some might say this is referring to the rapture before the tribulation since no one knows when that will happen.

In our study so far, Jesus did not teach of a rapture before the tribulation. All of His teaching is on signs leading up to His Second Coming. Signs meant for His followers, so they will be able to recognize the season in which He will return.

Pre-trib rapture believers seem to come at this from the opposite direction. They theorize that since Jesus gave us signs leading up to His Second Coming, and He gave us no signs leading up to the rapture, the rapture is the surprise, not Christ's Second Coming, because we can know the time of His Second Coming, based upon the seven year length of the tribulation.

There is a problem with that theory. Matthew 24:22 and Mark 13:20 tell us that unless the Lord had shortened those days (the days of the tribulation) no flesh would be saved; but for the elect's sake, whom He chose, He shortened the days. Therefore, we cannot know that the tribulation is precisely seven years long.

Regardless of how many years, months or days the tribulation lasts, we are told many times throughout God's Word that we are to watch and be ready. As Christians we can follow the signs Jesus has given us and know the season in which we live.

Chapter Three

STUDY IN CORINTHIANS

In I Corinthians, Chapter 15, Paul explains to us that the Risen or Resurrected Christ is our faith and our hope and through Him death will be destroyed. Paul goes on to explain the difference between our natural and spiritual bodies and that one day we will be changed.

The Risen Christ; Our Faith and Hope

1: **Moreover, brethren, I declare to you the gospel which I preached to you, which also you received and in which you stand,**

2: **by which also you are saved, if you hold fast that word which I preached to you - unless you believed in vain.**

3:      **For I delivered to you first of all that which I also received, that Christ died for our sins, according to the Scriptures,**

4:      **and that He was buried, and that He rose again the third day according to the Scriptures.**

If you believe the gospel as Paul preached to the Corinthians, that Christ is the Son of God, that He died for our sins, and that He rose again, then you are saved. We read in John 3:14-15, *"...even so must the Son of Man be lifted up, that whoever believes in Him should not perish but have eternal life."*

In Verses 5-11 Paul tells the Corinthians of some of the people who saw Christ after He was risen. We will go on to Verse 12. I Corinthians 15:

12:     **Now if Christ is preached that He has been raised from the dead, how do some among you say that there is no resurrection of the dead?**

13:     **But if there is no resurrection of the dead, then Christ is not risen.**

14:     **And if Christ is not risen, then our preaching is empty and your faith is also empty.**

In Verses 1-4 Paul told us our faith and salvation is based upon our belief that Christ, the Son of God, died for our sins and He rose on the third day. He said in Verse 2 "unless you believed in vain," meaning, as Verse 14 further explains, if Christ did not rise again, or if we do not believe He did, then we have nothing to base our faith on. Our faith is empty, or basically, we have no faith.

The words raised, rise and risen in Verses 12 through 14, and throughout Chapter 15, are from the Greek word EGEIRO, which means to waken, i.e., rouse (from sleep, from sitting or lying, from disease, from death). Lift up, raise up or again, rise up or again, stand, take up.

Resurrection is from the Greek word ANASTASIS, (from ANISTEMI) which means a standing up again, i.e., a resurrection from death, raised to life again, rise from the dead. ANISTEMI, means to stand up, arise, lift up, raise up, rise.

These words mean essentially the same thing so it would be correct to say either way; Christ was RAISED, or Christ was RESURRECTED.

15:   **Yes, and we are found false witnesses of God, because we have testified of God that He raised up Christ, who He did not raise up - if in fact the dead do not rise.**

16:   **For if the dead do not rise, then Christ is not risen.**

17:   **And if Christ is not risen, your faith is futile; you are still in your sins!**

18:   **Then also those who have fallen asleep in Christ have perished.**

19:   **If in this life only, we have hope in Christ, we are of all men the most pitiable.**

If Christ was raised, then the dead are raised. If the dead are not raised, then Christ was not raised. You have to believe both or neither.

If we do not believe that Christ was raised, then we cannot believe that the Christians who have died were raised, then we have no faith, (from Christ being raised), and we have no hope through Christ of our being raised.

The Resurrection of the Dead

20:   But now Christ is risen from the dead, and has become the firstfruits of those who have fallen asleep.

21:   For since by man came death, by Man also came the resurrection of the dead.

22:   For as in Adam all die, even so in Christ all shall be made alive.

23:   But each one in his own order. Christ the firstfruits, afterward those who are Christ's at His coming.

Through sin we have to die a physical death. Because Christ died to save us from our sins, and He was raised again, we can accept the gift of salvation through Christ and be raised to eternal life through Him.

Through Christ came the "resurrection of the dead", not the rapture of the dead. What does resurrection mean? The same thing as raised. But, when does this take place?

When are the Dead Raised?

We do believe that Christ was raised, so we must believe that the dead are raised, but when are they raised? In II Corinthians 5:6-8 we find out.

6:    So we are always confident, knowing that while we are at home in the body we are absent from the Lord.

7:    For we walk by faith, not by sight.

8:    We are confident, yes, well pleased rather to be absent from the body and to be present with the Lord.

While we are in our physical flesh body we are away from the presence of the Lord. When we die we are raised from our flesh body to our spiritual body and are in the presence of the Lord.

What does Verse 7 have to do with this? In the physical we cannot see that the dead are raised. We have to have faith that they are raised and therefore we will be also. This faith comes from believing in Christ and that He was raised from the dead.

Jude 14 tells us, concerning the Lord's return, *"...behold, the Lord comes with ten thousands of His saints."*

I Thessalonians 3:13 says, *"...at the coming of our Lord Jesus Christ with all His saints."*

If the saints have not been raised, how can they return with the Lord? Some might say these saints returning with the Lord are the Christians who have been raptured. The only problem with that (at least so far) is we have not read of a rapture, only a resurrection.

How Are the Dead Raised?

We have already determined when the dead are raised. When they are absent from their natural body they are present with the Lord. Starting with Verse 35 in I Corinthians 15, Paul tells us how the dead are raised and what kind of body they will have.

Also, we will find out later in the chapter when those of us who are still alive when Christ returns will be raised.

35:   **But someone will say, "How are the dead raised up? And with what body do they come?"**
36:   **Foolish one, what you sow is not made alive unless it dies.**
37:   **And what you sow, you do not sow that body that shall be, but mere grain - perhaps wheat or some other grain.**

What do you do when you sow? Plant. Paul uses this analogy to show us that if we die before Christ returns, and our body is "planted" or buried, it will not be the same body that is raised.

We discussed in Chapter One - Rapture, one of the teachings within the rapture theory is at the time of the rapture, the graves will be opened up and all the dead bodies of Christians who have died before the rapture will be gone. If the body we sow is not the body we will have when we are raised, then there would be no need for the bodies to be taken out of their graves.

Genesis 2:7, *"And the Lord God formed man of the dust of the ground, and breathed into his nostrils the breath of life; and man became a living being."*

Ecclesiastes 12:7 says, *"Then the dust will return to the earth as it was and the spirit will return to God who gave it."*

God made man from dust and our physical bodies return to dust. We will not need them anymore. We will have new bodies. Let's go back to I Corinthians 15.

What Kind of Body Will We Have?

38:   But God gives it a body as He pleases, and to each seed its own body.

39:   All flesh is not the same flesh, but there is one kind of flesh of men, another flesh of animals, another of fish, and another of birds.

40:   There are also celestial bodies and terrestrial bodies; but the glory of the celestial is one, and the glory of the terrestrial is another.

41:   There is one glory of the sun, another glory of the moon, and another glory of the stars, for one star differs from another star in glory.

There are different types of flesh and different types of bodies as well. The body we have now is not the same body we will have after Christ's return.

42:   So also is the resurrection of the dead. The body is sown in corruption, it is raised in incorruption.

43:   **It is sown in dishonor, it is raised in glory. It is sown in weakness, it is raised in power.**

44:   **It is sown a natural body, it is raised a spiritual body. There is a natural body, and there is a spiritual body.**

We will have a spiritual body instead of the natural body we have now. Our natural body will be raised from corruption, dishonor and weakness to incorruption, glory and power.

45:   **And so it is written, "The first man Adam became a living being." The last Adam became a life-giving spirit.**

46:   **However, the spiritual is not first, but the natural, and afterward the spiritual.**

47:   **The first man was of the earth, made of dust, the second Man is the Lord from heaven.**

48:   **As was the man of dust, so also are those who are made of dust; and as is the heavenly Man, so also are those who are heavenly.**

49:   **And as we have borne the image of the man of dust, we shall also bear the image of the heavenly Man.**

50:   **Now this I say, brethren, that flesh and blood cannot inherit the kingdom of God; nor does corruption inherit incorruption.**

Adam had a natural body, as we do now. The last Adam, Christ, became a life-giving Spirit with a spiritual body. As Paul explained in Verses 39-41 there are different kinds of bodies. We have a natural body first, then a spiritual body.

Our natural flesh and blood bodies cannot inherit the kingdom of God. They have to be raised from corruption, dishonor and weakness, from the natural to the spiritual.

When Are the Living Changed?

We have found, so far, that the dead will be raised from a natural body of corruption, dishonor and weakness to incorruption, glory and power; to a spiritual body. We have found out when this happens; when we are absent from our natural body we are present with the Lord in our spiritual body. But what about those of us who are still alive when Christ returns? When are we raised?

51:    **Behold, I tell you a mystery: We shall not all sleep, but we shall all be changed -**
52:    **in a moment, in the twinkling of an eye, at the last trumpet. For the trumpet will sound, and the dead will be raised incorruptible, and we shall be changed.**
53:    **For this corruptible must put on incorruption, and this mortal must put on immortality.**
54:    **So when this corruptible has put on incorruption, and this mortal has put on immortality, then shall be brought to pass the saying that is written: "Death is swallowed up to victory."**

In Paul's analogy of "planting" in Verse 36, he tells us that what you sow is not made alive unless it dies first. That is the mystery to which Paul is referring in Verse 51. There will be some who do not die before Christ returns, but we will be changed at His return to our spiritual bodies. That is to say, we will be raised to incorruption, glory and power, not raptured.

Chapter Four

STUDY IN THESSALONIANS

In Paul's first letter to the Thessalonians, in Chapter 4 beginning with Verse 13, Paul explains where our loved ones are who have died or will die a physical death before Christ returns. In the process of explaining this he gives a description of what will happen as our Lord returns. I Thessalonians 4:

Those Who Sleep in Jesus

13: **But I do not want you to be ignorant, brethren, concerning those who have fallen asleep, lest you sorrow as others who have no hope.**

14: For if we believe that Jesus died and rose again, even so God will bring with Him those who sleep in Jesus.

15: For this we say to you by the word of the Lord, that we who are alive and remain until the coming of the Lord will by no means precede those who are asleep.

Just as Jesus died and rose to be with the Father, so also have our fellow Christians who have died. As we have already learned from II Corinthians 5:6-8, when we are at home in the body we are absent from the Lord and when we are absent from the body we are present with the Lord.

Verse 14 says that God will bring the Christians with Him who have died a physical death. They have to be WITH Him for Him to be able to BRING them with Him.

To further explain Paul tells us that those of us who are living when the Lord returns will not go before the dead. They, like Jesus, have already risen to be with the Father, (or have been raised to their spiritual bodies) so we cannot precede them in being raised.

Is This the Rapture?

16: For the Lord Himself will descend from heaven with a shout, with the voice of an archangel, and with the trumpet of God. And the dead in Christ will rise first.

17:   **Then we who are alive and remain shall be caught up together with them in the clouds to meet the Lord in the air. And then we shall always be with the Lord.**
18:   **Therefore comfort one another with these words.**

As we have already learned in I Corinthians 15:52 the trumpet in Verse 16 is the LAST (seventh) trumpet. When the Lord comes again at the last trumpet, we will be gathered up to meet Him in the air. We will not be gathered until then.

Notice in Verse 17, we who are alive will be caught up together with THEM in the clouds. Who is "them"? "Them" are the ones who sleep in Jesus, who have already been raised and as Verse 14 tells us, God will bring them with Him.

Since Verse 17 is one of the main verses on which the rapture theory is based we need to make a study of this verse to see if this is what it is actually referring to. We will look at the key words in Verse 17 to see what they mean in the Greek language from which they were translated. We will then be able to determine whether or not this verse is describing being carried off to heaven.

We Shall Be Caught Up

CAUGHT - Caught is from the Greek word HARPAZO, which means to seize, (in various applications) catch (away, up) pluck, pull, take (by force). HARPAZO is derived from HAIREOMAI, which means to take for oneself, i.e., to prefer or choose. HAIREOMAI is akin to AIRO, a primary verb meaning to lift, take up or away, to raise.

In I Corinthians, Chapter 15, Paul explained that our natural body will be raised to a spiritual body. It is raised to incorruption over corruption, it is raised to glory over dishonor and it is raised to power over weakness.

Taking the word CAUGHT back to AIRO, the prime verb which means, for one, to raise up, we see how this ties in with our natural bodies being RAISED to spiritual bodies.

Together in the Clouds

CLOUD - Cloud is from NEPHELE, meaning a cloud or cloudiness. NEPHELE is derived from NEPHOS, a prime, meaning cloud. Neither of these specifies (as does the Hebrew words for cloud) whether these are clouds in the sky, such as nimbus or thunder clouds, or whether they have other meanings such as; to cover, to act covertly, or density.

In Hebrews 12:1 Paul says, *"Therefore we also, since we are surrounded by so great a CLOUD of witnesses..."* Taken in this context, one can conclude that Paul is referring to a group of people as opposed to a cloud in the sky.

I Thessalonians 4:14 says God will bring with Him those who sleep in Jesus. Jude 14 tells us the Lord will come with ten thousands of His saints. The Lord will return with His saints, which we would guess, judging from Jude 14, would be a very large group of people.

Keeping everything in context, we can see that the "clouds" in I Thessalonians 4:17 could easily refer to this group of people in the same way Paul used the word "cloud" in Hebrews 12:1 referring to a group of witnesses.

Meeting the Lord in the Air

AIR - Air is from AER, meaning to breathe, i.e., respire. The Word "air" as used in Matthew 8:20 *"...and birds of the AIR have nests..."* is from OURANOS, meaning the sky, heavens, air. AER is used in I Thessalonians 4:17, not OURANOS.

In I Corinthians 15 we read,

45:   And so it is written, the first man Adam became a living being. The last Adam became a life giving Spirit.
47:   The first man was of the earth, made of dust, the second Man is the Lord from heaven.

Our Lord is a "life giving Spirit". Genesis 2:7 tells us God breathed the "breath of life" into man.

As we found out, the word "air" in I Thessalonians 4:17 does not mean the sky, but rather, means to breathe. You can see then, how this ties in with I Corinthians 15:45 and 47. We will breathe the "breath of Life" from our Lord the "life giving Spirit".

Rapture or Resurrection?

After studying the key words of I Thessalonians 4:17 we could say: When the Lord returns we will be raised to our spiritual bodies by breathing the air of the life giving Spirit (meet the Lord in the air) and will gather together (be caught up) with the group of saints (in the clouds) that were already raised, as they return with the Lord.

As you can see, going back to the Greek for the actual meanings of the words used, as opposed to taking the literal English translation, gives us a totally different meaning then what is normally referred to as describing being seized and carried away to heaven.

It does not say we will be carried up to a cloud in the sky to meet Christ then be carried off to heaven. This does not give any confirmation to the rapture theory.

A Thief in the Night

We will continue in I Thessalonians, Chapter 5, where we are told to be alert and ready for the Lord's Second Coming. I Thessalonians 5:

1:    **But concerning the times and the seasons, brethren, you have no need that I would write to you.**

2:    **For you yourselves know perfectly that the day of the Lord so comes as a thief in the night.**

3:    For when they say "Peace and safety!" then
      sudden destruction comes upon them, as
      labor pains upon a pregnant woman. And
      they shall not escape.
4:    But you, brethren, are not in darkness, so
      that this Day should overtake you as a thief.
5:    You are all sons of light and sons of the day.
      We are not of the night nor of darkness.
6:    Therefore let us not sleep, as others do, but
      let us watch and be sober.

When the Lord comes again it will be a surprise
to some. It will be a surprise to the people who are of
the night, not to the people who are of the light.
Although we cannot know the exact day of our Lord's
return, Christians need not be surprised. In our study in
Matthew, Jesus gave us many signs (and warnings) of
things that will happen leading up to the end of the age
and His return.

We should be watchful and alert so we will
know the season in which we live. In Luke 21:28
Jesus says, *"Now when these things begin to happen,
look up and lift up your heads, because your
redemption draws near."*

If we are watchful and alert we will be able to
see these things begin to happen, and we will know
that the Lord's return is near. Therefore it will not
overtake us as a thief in the night.

Do Not Be Misled!

In Paul's second letter to the Thessalonians,
Chapter 2, he is concerned about their being confused

about the time of the Lord's Second Coming. He wants to make sure they realize that certain things must take place before the Lord returns. II Thessalonians 2:

1:   **Now, brethren, concerning the coming of our Lord Jesus Christ and our gathering together to Him, we ask you,**

2:   **not to be soon shaken in mind or troubled, either by spirit or by word or by letter, as if from us, as though the Day of Christ had come.**

We should not be misled or troubled if we hear someone say the Day of the Lord will come before certain things take place.

Paul ties together the Lord's Second Coming with the time when we are gathered together with Him. We have already established that the Lord returns at the last trumpet. It will be at that time, not before, when we are gathered together with Him. We need to know, regardless of what we may hear to the contrary, that the Lord will not return until certain things take place first.

Let's examine what must take place BEFORE the Day of the Lord comes.

3:   **Let no one deceive you by any means; for that Day will not come unless the falling away comes first, and the man of sin is revealed, the son of perdition,**

4:      who opposes and exalts himself above all that
        is called God or that is worshiped, so that he
        sits as God in the temple of God, showing
        himself that he is God.
5:      Do you not remember that when I was still
        with you I told you these things?

The Falling Away

Before our Lord returns there will be a great
falling away from God. The word "falling" is from the
Greek word APOSTASIA, meaning apostasy,
defection from truth.

II Timothy 4:3-4 (New Century Version) tells us
about some who defect from the truth.

3:      Because the time will come when people will
        not listen to the true teaching but will find
        many more teachers who please them by
        saying the things they want to hear.
4:      They will stop listening to the truth and will
        begin to follow false stories.

It may be pleasing to some to hear their pastor
or teacher tell them they will be raptured before the
tribulation, but is it the truth? Is it God's Word or is it a
false story?

The Son of Perdition

We are told also, that the man of sin, the son of
perdition must be revealed. Perdition means to perish.
There is only one that has already been judged to
perish, that is Satan. (You can read of this in Ezekiel,

Chapter 28.) Matthew 25:41 tells us where Satan has been judged to spend eternity, "...*Depart from Me, you cursed, into the everlasting fire prepared for the devil and his angels.*"

Revelation, Chapter 12, tells us how it will come about that the son of perdition is revealed. Revelation 12:

7:   And war broke out in heaven, Michael and his angels fought with the dragon, and the dragon and his angels fought,

8:   but they did not prevail, nor was a place found for them in heaven any longer.

9:   So the great dragon was cast out, that serpent of old, called the Devil and Satan, who deceives the whole world, he was cast to the earth, and his angels were cast out with him.

12:   ...Woe to the inhabitants of the earth and the sea. For the devil has come down to you, having great wrath, because he knows that he has a short time.

Christ will not return until the son of perdition, Satan, is revealed to us first. He will exalt himself above everything that is called God and show himself that he is God. This is what Jesus warned us about in Matthew. Satan will come before Christ and he will deceive many.

The Restrainer

Let's continue with our study in II Thessalonians, Chapter 2.

6:     **And now you know what is restraining, that he may be revealed in his own time.**

7:     **For the mystery of lawlessness is already at work; only He who now restrains will do so until He is taken out of the way.**

In Verse 6 we find that someone is restraining the son of perdition from being revealed until his own time. Some pre-trib rapture believers might conclude that the restrainer is the Holy Spirit.

The basis for this, according to the theory, is that when the Christians are raptured before the tribulation the Holy Spirit is taken as well since He abides in Christians (Romans 8:11). Therefore they say, the Holy Spirit must be the restrainer, since taking Him to heaven with the Christians will allow the son of perdition to be revealed.

First, nowhere in the above verses is there any mention of the Holy Spirit being the restrainer. Second, from what we have studied so far, there is no mention of Christians being raptured before the tribulation. Rather, we were given signs and warnings of the things that must happen before Christ returns.

We were told to be alert and watchful and to lift up our heads when we see these things begin to happen because our redemption is near. Nowhere in our study have we been told that we will not experience the things that will occur before our Lord returns.

This certainly sounds as if Christians will be here through the tribulation. If Christians will be here, so then will the Holy Spirit; therefore He cannot be the restrainer.

It could be possible that the restrainer is Michael. As we just read in Revelation 12:7-9, Michael fought with Satan and he was cast out of heaven. Also, we read of Michael in Daniel 12:

1:   At that time Michael shall stand up, the great prince who stands watch over the sons of your people; and there shall be a time of trouble, such as never was since there was a nation, even to that time.

The word "restraining" in II Thessalonians 2:6 means to hold or to hold down. The word "stand" in Daniel 12:1 has several applications but can mean to cease or to stand still. If Michael is now holding or restraining Satan, then ceases to do so, or stands still, at which time the trouble begins, one could by this speculate that the restrainer is Michael.

Michael being the restrainer is of course speculation but, I do not believe that knowing exactly who the restrainer is would be vital to our salvation. What is important though is knowing that the son of perdition WILL BE REVEALED, and that this will take place BEFORE Christ returns.

Satan will sit as God, in the temple of God, showing himself that he is God. He will perform great signs and wonders and will deceive many. It is important for us to know all of this so we will not be deceived into worshipping the wrong "Christ".

Chapter Five

STUDY IN REVELATION

W e will not be examining any one particular chapter in Revelation as we did in the other Books, but rather, we are going to look at several different verses throughout Revelation that have been used by rapture theorists to support their viewpoint.

Before we get into that though, we would like to make one point in regard to the Book of Revelation.

Do You Know What Must Shortly Take Place?

Too often we are told by pastors and teachers of the Word of God, who adhere to the rapture theory, that we do not need to read or understand the Book of Revelation because we are not going to be here anyway. We will be gone in the rapture. We do not need to know what will happen through the tribulation, or who the anti-christ will be, because we are not going to be here.

Inasmuch as I realize that this way of thinking is propagated from their belief in the rapture theory, we need to consider someone else's viewpoint: God's.

Reading Revelation 1:1-3 should clear this up for us.

1:    **The Revelation of Jesus Christ, which God gave Him to show His servants - things which must shortly take place. And He sent and signified it by His angel to His servant John,**

2:    **who bore witness to the Word of God, and to the testimony of Jesus Christ, to all things that he saw.**

3:    **Blessed is he who reads and those who hear the words of this prophecy, and keep those things which are written in it; for the time is near.**

God gave the Revelation to Jesus Christ to show His servants the things which must shortly take place. Apparently, if you are not a servant of Jesus Christ you do not have a need to read the Revelation.

We believe it is clear to those of us who are servants, that God Himself who handed this Revelation down, wants us to read the Revelation and to know the things which must shortly take place. Verse 3 really magnifies this in that it tells us the ones who read and hear the words of this prophecy, the Revelation, and keep the things which are written in it are blessed.

Our point: Read the Book of Revelation!

Past, Present, Future

Now, we will go on with our study in Revelation concerning the rapture theory.

John is told in Revelation 1:

19:    **"Write the things which you have seen, and the things which are, and the things which will take place after this."**

Because of this verse, Revelation has been divided, by man, into three parts. Chapter 1 being "the things which you have seen" or the past. Chapters 2 and 3, "the things which are", the present. And, Chapters 4 through 22, "the things which will take place after this", the future.

Because of this division, rapture theory believers theorize that since the Church is not mentioned after Revelation, Chapter 3 (except, they say, in Revelation 4:1: the Church being called to Heaven in the rapture) or in the "future" chapters, this must mean the Church will not be here during the things which must shortly take place, or through the tribulation.

Concerning the division of the Book of Revelation, we would like to present another viewpoint.

Revelation, Chapters 2 and 3 are the messages that Jesus Christ gave to John to write to the churches. It is true that the seven churches were actual, literal churches in John's time, which would be "the things which are" or the present, to John. It is also true that Revelation, Chapters 4 through 22 deal with prophecy, which would be "the things which will take place" or the future, to John.

It is also taught that the seven churches represent seven periods of time, or church ages, from the time of Christ until today. Be that as it may, the question we need to address at this point is: What is the significance of the letters to the churches to us today? Were they just put there so we could divide the Book of Revelation? Was it so we could assume that when John finished addressing the churches, then does not mention them again, that they (we, as the Church) are just carried off to heaven? We do not think so.

We believe that we were given the letters to the churches as examples of both how we should live our lives individually and how we should operate collectively, as the Church, in the service of our Lord.

Inasmuch as the Book of Revelation deals with prophecy, if we stick to the subject, it could be said that we were given the letters to the churches as examples of how to live and operate as we see, and go through, the things which must shortly take place.

There may be many who would disagree with this viewpoint. So be it. At the least, it is something you might think about.

Kept From the Hour of Trial

Some pre-trib rapture believers use this next verse to prove that God is going to take the Church out of the world before the tribulation. Revelation 3:

10:   **"Because you have kept My command to persevere, I also will keep you from the hour of trial which shall come upon the whole world, to test those who dwell on the earth."**

The word "from" in this verse is used as the key word by pre-trib rapture theorists. "From" is from the Greek word EK which means, they say, "out of", meaning then that the Church will be kept from the hour of trial by being taken "out of" the world via the rapture.

The Greek word EK is a prime denoting origin (the point when motion or action proceeds). Some examples explaining the use of this word are: from, out, after, off, on, among, since and through. It does not mean "out of" as in carried away.

"From the hour of trial" is explaining WHAT we will be kept from, not HOW we are kept from it.

The word "keep" is the word that explains to us HOW we are kept from the hour of trial. "Keep" is from the Greek word TEREO, which means to watch, to guard (from loss or injury, by keeping an eye on). This differs from "keep" that is from the Greek word PHULASSO meaning isolation, to prevent or to escape.

So, what Revelation 3:10 tells us is the Lord will guard us or watch out for us as we go through the hour of trial or the tribulation.

In John 17:15 Jesus is praying for His disciples. He says, *"I do not pray that You should take them out of the world, but that You should keep them from the evil one."* The word "keep" in this verse is also from TEREO, meaning to watch over or to guard. Jesus did not ask that they escape the evil one via a rapture, but rather, that they be protected from him.

In the next chapter we will look at some examples given to us in God's Word of the Lord watching over His servants. For now though, let's examine another verse that supposedly depicts the rapture.

"Come Up Here"

Another verse used to try to substantiate the pre-trib theory is Revelation 4:1. Some pre-trib theorists say Revelation 4:1 must be the rapture of the Church because the Church is not mentioned again after this, meaning the Church will not go through the tribulation. Supposedly, the "Come up here" is Jesus calling the Church up to Heaven. Revelation 4:

1:   **After these things I looked, and behold, a door standing open in heaven. And the first voice which I heard was like a trumpet speaking with me, saying, "Come up here, and I will show you things which must take place after this."**

As we learned in Revelation 1:1, Jesus Christ handed down the Revelation to John to write. If you leave Revelation 4:1 in context and follow the subject, it is very clear that Jesus Christ is talking to John, and only John, telling him to "come up here" so He could show him the things which must shortly take place.

In Revelation 22:8 we see that John did in fact see these things. Revelation 22:

8:   **Now I, John, saw and heard these things. And when I heard and saw, I fell down to worship before the feet of the angel who showed me these things.**

Inasmuch as Revelation 4:1 begins the future "division" of the Book of Revelation, it is used to prove the timing of the rapture as well as the rapture itself. Since Chapters 4 through 22 describe future events (the time of sorrows, the great tribulation, and our Lord's return), and the rapture is described in Verse 1 of Chapter 4, this proves, they say, that the rapture takes place before all of the future events take place.

The problem with the timing aspect is this: Revelation 4:1 does not say anything to or about the

Church. Jesus Christ calls John up to Heaven to show him what must shortly take place. This does not prove the rapture theory and therefore cannot establish the timing of the rapture either.

Who Are the Two Witnesses?

Concerning the Church not being mentioned after Revelation 4:1, we want to look at Revelation 11:

3:    **"And I will give power to my two witnesses, and they will prophesy one thousand two hundred and sixty days, clothed in sackcloth."**

4:    **These are the two olive trees and the two lampstands standing before the God of the earth.**

Before proceeding we want to say, there are some who believe that the two witnesses are either Moses and Elijah or Enoch and Elijah. We are not going to go into why they believe this nor is it our intention in approaching this subject to refute their interpretation. We intend simply to share with you our understanding of whom the two witnesses may represent.

The two witnesses are the TWO olive trees and the TWO lampstands. Often in God's Word, the number two is related to witnessing. Here are a few examples:

16:    **"But if he will not hear, take with you one or two more, that by the mouth of two or three witnesses every word may be established."**

Matthew 18

19:     **Do not receive an accusation against an elder except from two or three witnesses.**

I Timothy 5

7:      **And He called the twelve to Himself, and began to send them out two by two, and gave them power over unclean spirits.**

12:     **So they went out and preached that people should repent.**

Mark 6

These verses seem to be referring to two individuals as witnesses, but because the olive trees and the lampstands are symbols, it could be that they represent groups of people as witnesses, not necessarily just two individuals.

The Two Olive Trees

In Romans 11:11-27 Paul refers to the Gentiles as a wild olive tree and to Israel as a cultivated olive tree. Romans 11:24 reads:

24:     **For if you (Gentiles) were cut out of the olive tree which is wild by nature, and were grafted contrary to nature into a cultivated olive tree, how much more will these (Israel), who are natural branches, be grafted into their own olive tree?**

Could the two olive trees in Revelation 11:4 represent the two olive trees spoken of by Paul?

In Zechariah, Chapter 4, Zechariah has a vision of the lampstand and the two olive trees. Zechariah 4:

11:     Then I answered and said to him, "What are
        these two olive trees - at the right of the
        lampstand and at its left?"
14:     So he said, "These are the two anointed ones,
        who stand beside the Lord of the whole
        earth."

The word "anointed", as used here means to
glisten, as producing light.

Jesus, speaking of believers, says in Matthew 5:

14:     "You are the light of the world. A city that is
        set on a hill cannot be hidden."
15:     "Nor do they light a lamp and put it under a
        basket, but on a lampstand, and it gives light
        to all who are in the house."
16:     "Let your light so shine before men, that
        they may see your good works and glorify
        your Father in heaven."

The two olive trees are the two anointed ones.
The anointed ones produce light. Believers are the light
of the world.

The Two Lampstands

The lampstands are explained in Revelation
1:20, "...the seven lampstands which you saw are the
seven churches." In the Word of God the number seven
represents completeness or Spiritual perfection.

In Mark 13:9b we read, "You will be brought
before rulers and kings for My sake, for a testimony to
them." Believers will be brought before rulers and
kings to be used as witnesses for our Lord.

In Revelation 11:3 we read that the two witnesses will prophesy. We read of this again in Joel 2 referring to the Latter days. Joel 2:

28:   **And it shall come to pass afterward that I will pour out My Spirit on all flesh; your sons and your daughters shall prophesy, your old men shall dream dreams, your young men shall see visions.**

29:   **And also on My menservants and on My maidservants I will pour out My Spirit in those days.**

Could it be said then, that the two witnesses (the number two in God's Word relating to witnessing) represent the Church, the body of believers?

IF the two witnesses represent the Church, then not only are we mentioned after Revelation 4:1 (of which the pre-trib belief maintains to be the rapture), but it would seem that we have an important role in the events of the last days.

The Two Witnesses Are Raised Up

In Revelation 11:11-15 we read of the two witnesses, whoever they may be, RAISED UP or RESURRECTED at Christ's return. Revelation 11:

11:   **Now after the three-and-a-half days the breath of life from God entered them, and they stood on their feet, and great fear fell on those who saw them.**

12:    And they heard a loud voice from heaven saying to them, "Come up here." And they ascended to heaven in a cloud, and their enemies saw them.

13:    In the same hour there was a great earthquake, and a tenth of the city fell. In the earthquake seven thousand people were killed, and the rest were afraid and gave glory to the God of heaven.

14:    The second woe is past. Behold, the third woe is coming quickly.

15:    Then the seventh angel sounded: And there were loud voices in heaven, saying, "The kingdoms of this world have become the kingdoms of our Lord and of His Christ, and He shall reign forever and ever!"

The Resurrection takes place at Christ's return as the seventh angel sounds his trumpet and the kingdoms of the world become the Lord's.

In I Thessalonians 4:17 we learned that the word "air" means to breathe. We are raised up by breathing the breath of life from God (Revelation 11:11). Those who have already died and risen to be with the Lord will return with Him (I Thessalonians 4:14 and Jude 14). I Corinthians 15:52 tells us this will occur at the last or seventh trumpet as Christ returns (Revelation 11:15).

Also, at the last trumpet, those of us who are still alive (in our natural bodies) will be changed and gather together in the clouds to meet the Lord (I Corinthians 15:51, I Thessalonians 4:17 and Revelation 11:12).

The First Resurrection

Now let's turn to Revelation 19:

11:   Now I saw heaven opened, and behold, a white horse. And He who sat on him was called Faithful and True, and in righteousness He judges and makes war.

12:   His eyes were like a flame of fire, and on His head were many crowns. He had a name written that no one knew except Himself.

13:   He was clothed with a robe dipped in blood, and His name is called The Word of God.

14:   And the armies in heaven, clothed in fine linen, white and clean, followed him on white horses.

15:   Now out of His mouth goes a sharp sword, that with it He should strike the nations. And He Himself will rule them with a rod of iron. He Himself treads the winepress of the fierceness and wrath of Almighty God.

16:   And He has on His robe and on His thigh a name written: King of kings and Lord of lords.

This describes the Lord's Second Coming as He sets up His one thousand year rule and reign on earth as the King of kings and Lord of lords.

The armies, in Verse 14, who follow the Lord on white horses are the saints, who have died a physical death before His return, and have already risen to be with the Lord. How do we know these armies are the saints? Revelation 19:7-8 tells us.

7:      **"Let us be glad and rejoice and give Him
        glory, for the marriage of the Lamb has
        come, and His wife has made herself ready."**
8:      **And to her it was granted to be arrayed in
        fine linen, clean and bright, for the fine linen
        is the righteous acts of the saints.**

The armies following Christ are clothed in fine linen, white and clean.

They follow the Lord. Where? To earth, to set up His kingdom. Verse 15 says the Lord will strike the nations with a sharp sword that goes out of His mouth (the Word of God) and He will rule them. Where are the nations? On earth.

Keeping in line with the subject, which is Christ's return to earth and the events that will transpire at that time, Revelation 20:1-3 tells us that Satan, upon Christ's return, will be bound and cast into the bottomless pit, where he will stay for the one thousand year reign of Christ. Then he will be let loose for a little while. Let's continue reading in Revelation 20.

4:      **And I saw thrones, and they sat on them, and
        judgment was committed to them. Then I
        saw the souls of those who had been
        beheaded for their witness to Jesus and for
        the Word of God, who had not worshiped the
        beast or his image, and had not received his
        mark on their foreheads or on their hands.
        And they lived and reigned with Christ for a
        thousand years.**

5:    But the rest of the dead did not live again
      until the thousand years were finished. This
      is the first resurrection.

6:    Blessed and holy is he who has part in the
      first resurrection. Over such the second
      death has no power, but they shall be priests
      of God and of Christ, and shall reign with
      Him a thousand years.

Remember the subject? Christ's return. John sees the souls of those who will live and reign with Christ for one thousand years. Where does Christ reign for one thousand years? On earth. Who are these souls that John sees on earth, living and reigning with Christ and how did they come to be with Christ? Were they raptured?

The ones who died a physical death before Christ's return followed Him back to earth (Revelation 19:14). The ones who are alive when Christ returns are raised to their spiritual bodies (I Corinthians 15:51-52). Verse 5 says, "This is the first RESURRECTION," not rapture.

Chapter Six

WHO IS LEAVING FIRST?

W e have heard it taught that the following verses of Scripture are referring to the rapture. We have heard Christians say they want to be first in line for the rapture, that they want to be among the first taken. Jesus tells us in Luke 17 about the first ones taken. Luke 17:

Gathered to the Dead Body

34: "I tell you, in that night there will be two men in one bed: the one will be taken and the other will be left."

35: "Two women will be grinding together: the one will be taken and the other left."

36: "Two men will be in the field: the one will be taken and the other left."

37: And they answered and said to Him, "Where, Lord?" So He said to them, "Wherever the body is, there the eagles will be gathered together."

The New Century Version gives a better translation of Verse 37.

37: Jesus answered, "Where there is a dead body, there the vultures will gather."

We could relate this "dead body" to Satan, since he had the power of death and he is the only one who has already been judged to perish. Hebrews 2:

14: Inasmuch then as the children have partaken of flesh and blood, He Himself likewise shared in the same, that through death He might destroy him who had the power of death, that is, the devil.

We still have to die a physical death, but if we accept salvation through Christ the second death (spiritual) will have no power over us as it will Satan. He will not escape the second death as we read in Revelation 20:

10: The devil, who deceived them, was cast into the lake of fire and brimstone where the beast and the false prophet are. And they will be tormented day and night forever and ever.

14: Then Death and Hades were cast into the lake of fire. This is the second death.

The gathering to a dead body is used as an analogy to say there will be people who have been deceived into believing that Satan, when he is cast down to earth, is the real Christ, and they will gather to him. They have been misled. They have been told that Christ is coming first to rapture them away.

When Satan comes presenting himself as "Christ" and performing great signs and wonders, people will be deceived and follow after him. The first ones to leave gather to Satan.

Parable of the Tares

Again, let's see if we can determine what happens to the first ones taken. Matthew 13:

24: **Another parable He put forth to them, saying: "The kingdom of heaven is like a man who sowed good seed in his field;"**

25: **"but while men slept, his enemy came and sowed tares among the wheat and went his way."**

26: **"But when the grain had sprouted and produced a crop, then the tares also appeared."**

27: **"So the servants of the owner came and said to him, 'Sir, did you not sow good seed in your field?' How then does it have tares?"**

28: **"He said to them. An enemy has done this. The servants said to him. 'Do you want us then to go and gather them up?'"**

29: **"But he said, 'No, lest while you gather up the tares you also uproot the wheat with them.'"**

30:    "Let both grow together until the harvest,
       and at the time of harvest I will say to the
       reapers, 'First gather together the tares and
       bind them in bundles to burn them, but
       gather the wheat into my barn.'"

The tares are gathered first to be burned. You
might be wondering what this has to do with the
subject. Let's find out as Jesus explains the parable.
Matthew 13:

36:    ...And His disciples came to Him, saying,
       "Explain to us the parable of the tares of the
       field."
37:    He answered and said to them: "He who
       sows the good seed is the Son of Man."
38:    "The field is the world, the good seeds are
       the sons of the kingdom, but the tares are the
       sons of the wicked one."
39:    "The enemy who sowed them is the devil, the
       harvest is the end of the age, and the reapers
       are the angels."
40:    "Therefore as the tares are gathered and
       burned in the fire, so it will be at the end of
       this age."
41:    "The Son of Man will send out His angels,
       and they will gather out of His kingdom all
       things that offend, and those who practice
       lawlessness,"
42:    "and will cast them into the furnace of fire.
       There will be wailing and gnashing of teeth."
43:    "Then the righteous will shine forth as the
       sun in the kingdom of their Father. He who
       has ears to hear, let him hear!"

Christ sows the good seed who are His sons, the sons of the kingdom. Satan sows the bad seed and they are his sons, the sons of the wicked one.

The harvest is the end of the age. The sons of the wicked one will be gathered first, at the end of this age. The angels are sent to gather everything that offends OUT of the kingdom, leaving the righteous to shine forth.

Do not be misled. Satan comes before Christ. He will deceive many. Many will gather to him thinking he is Christ and has come to rapture them away. Jesus warned us of this deception many times. Christ's kingdom will be here on earth. The sons of the wicked one will be gathered out of it.

The Faithful Servant

Are you a faithful servant? Luke 12:

37:   "Blessed are those servants whom the master, when he comes, will find watching. Assuredly, I say to you that he will gird himself and have them sit down to eat, and will come and serve them."

38:   "And if he should come in the second watch, or come in the third watch, and find them so, blessed are those servants."

39:   "But know this, that if the master of the house had known what hour the thief would come, he would have watched and not allowed his house to be broken into."

40:   "Therefore you also be ready, for the Son of Man is coming at an hour you do not expect."

One of the points of pre-trib rapturism is imminency. Some call it the "any moment" doctrine. That is to say that at any moment the rapture could occur.

We are told to be watchful so we will know the season in which our Lord returns. If the rapture is imminent, and there are no signs given or events that must precede it, how then can we be watchful? What are we to watch? The signs Jesus gave leading up to the end of the age.

We have seen that nobody is gathered from the field, or the world, until the harvest, which Jesus said was the end of the age. The ones who are gathered from the field are the sons of the wicked one.

As Luke 12:37-40 above tells us, Jesus wants us to watch and be ready for His return. He even gives us a warning of what will happen if we do not watch. Revelation 3:

3:   "Remember therefore how you have received and heard; hold fast and repent. Therefore if you will not watch, I will come upon you as a thief, and you will now know what hour I will come upon you."

A faithful servant watches and is ready for Christ's return. Jesus said the servants that He finds "watching" upon His return are blessed.

Not only are we told to be watchful but also to continue in the Lord's work until He returns. Continuing in Luke 12:

42:   And the Lord said, "Who then is that faithful and wise steward, whom his master will make ruler over his household, to give them their portion of food in due season?"

43:   "Blessed is that servant whom his master will find so doing when he comes."

44:   "Truly, I say to you that he will make him ruler over all that he has."

The servant who continues in the work of the Lord is said to be faithful, wise and blessed, and he will be made a ruler. We see also in Matthew 28 that we are to continue in His work. Matthew 28:

19:   "Go therefore and make disciples of all the nations, baptizing them in the name of the Father and of the Son and of the Holy Spirit,"

20:   "teaching them to observe all things that I have commanded you; and lo, I am with you always, even to the end of the age."

We are told to spread the Gospel to the end of the age, not to the rapture. A faithful servant is one who continues in the service of the Lord until He returns, not the one who leaves first so they will not miss out on being raptured.

Do you have ears to hear? Do you want to be one of the first ones to leave?

Chapter Seven

GOD'S PROTECTION

In our study in Revelation, within the letter to the church of Philadelphia, (Revelation 3:10) we learned that they will be kept from the hour of trial. This promise was not made to any of the other churches. Let's review that letter in it's entirety to see if we can determine why Christ said He would watch over the Philadelphians. Revelation 3:

7:     "And to the angel of the church of Philadelphia write, 'These things says He who is holy. He who is true. He who has the key of David. He who opens and no one shuts, and shuts and no one opens.'"

8:    "I know your works. See, I have set before you an open door, and no one can shut it; for you have a little strength, have kept My word, and have not denied My name."

9:    "Indeed I will make those of the synagogue of Satan, who say they are Jews and are not, but lie - indeed I will make them come and worship before your feet, and to know that I have loved you."

10:    "Because you have kept My command to persevere, I also will keep you from the hour of trial which shall come upon the whole world, to test those who dwell on the earth."

11:    "Behold, I am coming quickly! Hold fast what you have, that no one may take your crown."

12:    "He who overcomes, I will make him a pillar in the temple of My God, and he shall go out no more. I will write on him the name of My God and the name of the city of My God, the New Jerusalem, which comes down out of heaven from My God. And I will write on him My new name."

13:    "He who has an ear, let him hear what the Spirit says to the churches."

The Philadelphians 1.) have a little strength, 2.) have kept His Word, 3.) have not denied His name and 4.) have kept His command to persevere. The King James Version translates persevere as patience, meaning endurance or constancy.

Why Philadelphia?

Some might say the reason Jesus told the church of Philadelphia that He would keep them from the hour of trial would be obvious in Verse 10, *"because you have kept My command to persevere."* The problem with this is that Jesus commended two of the other churches on their patience as well without telling them that He would keep them from the hour of trial.

Jesus said of the church of Philadelphia that they did not deny His name, but He also said of one other church that they *"hold fast to My name."*

Although we should of course not deny His name and we should keep His command of patience, the key, quite possibly, is in the observance of ALL FOUR of the things on which Jesus commended the church of Philadelphia.

Besides not denying His name and keeping His command of patience the Philadelphians had a little strength. Strength here means "being able" or "can do". To quote one of the best teachers the Lord has given us, he says, "Our Father likes 'can do' type people." Apparently He does.

Most importantly, Jesus said, you *"have kept My word."* What does God's Word consist of? There is a lot more to God's Word than the message of salvation. For someone who is not born again, that is the most important part, but it is only the beginning.

There is also a lot more to God's Word than the command to persevere. Do we know what God's Word says? Do we know what His commands are? We cannot know what God's Word says nor KEEP His Word unless we read and study it.

The importance of this is that there will be some who are kept from the hour of trial. They are clearly the ones who keep God's Word and commands and do not deny His name. God will not keep these people from the hour of trial via a rapture. We have found no evidence of that in our study.

Just as He kept Noah, Daniel, and Shadrach, Meshach and Abed-Nego (to name just a few) from harm, not by a rapture, but by providing Divine protection because of their faith in Him, their obedience to Him and their willingness to heed His warnings, He will also in this way keep you from harm.

We will find in reading the accounts of Noah, Daniel, and Shadrach, Meshach and Abed-Nego that there is a common factor. Let's see if we can find out what that is.

Noah Keeps God's Commands

In Genesis, Chapters 6-8, we find the account of Noah and his family being kept from the destruction of the flood. Noah was found to be a just and righteous man in God's eyes. This means he kept God's Word and His commands.

In Chapter 6, Verses 13-21, God tells Noah how to prepare for himself and his family to survive the flood. Verse 22 of that same chapter says, *"Thus Noah did; according to all God commanded him, so he did."*

We see that Noah SERVED God; he kept His commands, both throughout his life and in preparation for the flood. God did not rapture him off the earth, but rather kept him from harm as he went through the flood.

Shadrach, Meshach and Abed-Nego

In Daniel, Chapter 3, we read of Shadrach, Meshach and Abed-Nego being thrown into a burning fiery furnace because they would not worship King Nebuchadnezzar's gold image. Daniel 3:

14: **Nebuchadnezzar spoke, saying to them, "Is it true Shadrach, Meshach and Abed-Nego, that you do not serve my gods or worship the gold image which I have set up?"**

15b: **"But if you do not worship you shall be cast immediately into the midst of a burning fiery furnace. And who is the god who will deliver you from my hands?"**

17: **"If that is the case, our God whom we serve is able to deliver us from the burning fiery furnace, and He will deliver us from your hand, O King."**

They tell the king that the God whom they SERVE is able to deliver them from the burning furnace. They have no doubt about it; they have faith and do not deny His name. Continuing in Daniel 3:

22: **Therefore, because the king's command was urgent, and the furnace exceedingly hot, the flame of the fire killed those men who took up Shadrach, Meshach, and Abed-Nego.**

The king had ordered the furnace turned up to seven times hotter than normal. (Verse 19) It was so hot it killed the men throwing them into the furnace.

This shows us that regardless of the circumstance affecting someone standing right next to you, you can be protected by God's Divine protection.

25:     "Look!" he answered, "I see four men loose, walking in the midst of the fire; and they are not hurt, and the form of the fourth is like the Son of God."

26a: Then Nebuchadnezzar went near the mouth of the burning furnace and spoke, saying, "Shadrach, Meshach, and Abed-Nego, servants of the Most High God, come out, and come here."

27:     ...and they saw these men on whose bodies the fire had no power; the hair of their head was not singed nor were their garments affected, and the smell of fire was not on them.

28:     Nebuchadnezzar spoke, saying, "Blessed be the God of Shadrach, Meshach, and Abed-Nego, who sent His Angel and delivered His servants who trusted in Him..."

The Son of God walked with the three keeping them from harm. They did not even *smell* like smoke. Notice in Verse 28 the king now recognizes that these three are SERVANTS of the Most High God and that they trust in Him. They have faith in Him as we should have that He can protect us from whatever comes against us, even the events during the tribulation.

Daniel in the Lion's Den

In Daniel, Chapter 6, we read of Daniel being thrown into the lion's den because he would not stop serving God for thirty days. Daniel 6:

16:   So the king gave the command, and they brought Daniel and cast him into the den of lions. But the king spoke, saying to Daniel, "Your God, whom you serve continually, He will deliver you."

The king knew that Daniel was a SERVANT of God. He served Him continually and because of this God would protect him.

20b: The king spoke, saying to Daniel, "Daniel, servant of the living God, has your God, whom you serve continually, been able to deliver you from the lions?"

22:   "My God sent His angel and shut the lions' mouths, so that they have not hurt me, because I was found innocent before Him..."

23b: So Daniel was taken up out of the den, and no injury whatever was found on him, because he believed in his God.

Daniel believed in God for protection, not a rapture. God did not rapture him out of the lion's den, He left him in the lion's den and provided him with protection.

In all three of these examples that God has set forth for us the subject has served God, kept His commands, and believed in, trusted and had faith in Him.

If we expect God to keep us from the coming hour of trial, as he promised in His letter to the church of Philadelphia, we need to do our part. We need to do what the church of Philadelphia was doing. We should follow the examples. Keep His Word, and keep His commands.

Guarded From the Evil One

Jesus did not expect us to be snatched away from tribulation, but prayed for our protection through it. His prayer in John 17:

15:   "I do not pray that You should take them out of the world, but that You should keep them from the evil one."

The word "keep" in John 17:15 means the same as the word "keep" in Revelation 3:10; to watch over or to guard.

Paul writes in 2 Thessalonians 3:

3:   But the Lord is faithful, who will establish you and guard you from the evil one.

The word "establish", as used here means to strengthen. The Lord will strengthen you and guard you from the evil one.

God's Wrath

Some might say, "Well, maybe you have a point concerning protection through the tribulation, but what about God's wrath? We have to be raptured then because God would not let us go through that."

God did not appoint His children to wrath as we read in the following verses.

9:      For God did not appoint us to wrath, but to
        obtain salvation through our Lord Jesus
        Christ.

                              I Thessalonians 5

36:     "He who believes in the Son has everlasting
        life; and he who does not believe the Son
        shall not see life, but the wrath of God abides
        on him."

                                        John 3

9:      Much more then, having now been justified
        by His blood, we shall be saved from wrath
        through Him.

                                      Romans 5

If we believe in God's Son, Jesus Christ, we will
obtain salvation, being justified by His blood and thus
be saved from the wrath of God. "Saved" means to
deliver or to protect. We have been granted God's
protection from wrath.

Who is Appointed to Wrath?

Let's look at some verses of Scripture to see
what the Lord is going to do at His return. We will
start with Isaiah 13:

9:      Behold, the day of the Lord comes, cruel,
        with both wrath and fierce anger, to lay the
        land desolate; and He will destroy its sinners
        from it.

10:    I will punish the world for its evil, and the
       wicked for their iniquity; I will halt the
       arrogance of the proud, and will lay low the
       haughtiness of the terrible.

He is going to destroy the sinners FROM the
land. He is going to punish the world and the wicked.
The punishment is not meant for Christians. We are
not of the world as Jesus explains in John 15:

19:    "If you were of the world, the world would
       love it's own. Yet because you are not of the
       world, but I chose you out of the world,
       therefore the world hates you."

Let's continue reading some verses to see what
the Lord will do upon His return and for whom this
punishment is meant.

14:    ...Behold, the Lord comes with ten thousands
       of His saints,
15:    to execute judgment on all, to convict all who
       are ungodly among them of all their ungodly
       deeds which they have committed in an
       ungodly way, and of all the harsh things
       which ungodly sinners have spoken against
       Him.

                                          Jude

18:    For the wrath of God is revealed from
       heaven against all ungodliness and
       unrighteousness of men, who suppress the
       truth in unrighteousness.

                                       Romans 1

**18:   The nations were angry, and Your wrath has
come, and the time of the dead, that they
should be judged, and that You should
reward Your servants the prophets and the
saints, and those who fear Your name, small
and great, and should destroy those who
destroy the earth.**

Revelation 11

He is going to execute judgment on the ungodly
and the unrighteous and destroy those who destroy the
earth, but at the same time reward those who serve
Him. We read of this again in Matthew 16:

**27:   For the Son of Man will come in the glory of
His Father with His angels, and then He will
reward each according to his works.**

If you do not fit into the category of the ungodly
or the unrighteous then there is nothing to worry about,
the wrath of God is not meant for you. If you are a
servant of God then you will be rewarded as such.

Fire, Hail and Plagues

Some might say, "You still do not understand.
What about the fire and the hail and the plagues? Why
would God leave us here to go through all of that?"

That is exactly why God set forth the examples
in His Word of His Divine protection. He gave Noah
instruction on how to survive the flood. He closed the
lion's mouths for Daniel. Shadrach, Meshach and

Abed-Nego walked through the fire without being touched. He protected Israel from the plagues that came upon Egypt.

God will protect His servants in the end-times just as He did in the past. God loves His children. His wrath is not aimed at us. He is even in control of Satan's wrath upon this earth. We should be able to take comfort in knowing that our Father is in control.

We should have faith that He is capable of protecting us and trust that He will IF we put our faith and trust in Him rather than in a tradition that has it's origin little more than 150 years ago and cannot be found in God's Word.

Chapter Eight

NEW BEGINNINGS

In Matthew we learned of the time of sorrows. This time will include wars, famines, earthquakes, pestilences, increased lawlessness and deception. We will see the abomination of desolation, after which there will be a time of great tribulation. The Gospel will be preached to every nation. Christ will not return until after all of these things take place. But, if we keep our faith in God and endure until the end we will be saved.

In Corinthians we learned that when we die we are raised to our spiritual bodies and go to be with the Lord. We learned what our spiritual bodies are like and how we are changed. Those of us who are living at

Christ's return will not die a physical death, but will immediately be raised from our physical bodies to our spiritual bodies. We learned that Christ returns at the sound of the last trumpet.

In Thessalonians we learned of the apostasy and the revealing of the son of perdition that will occur before Christ's return. We learned where our loved ones are who have already died a physical death, or will, before Christ returns. All those who sleep in Christ will return with Him.

We learned of the ones who are taken first and what happens to them. We learned that some will be kept from the hour of trial by God watching over them and guarding them. We learned of God's protection of His servants. We learned that we will not be gathered back to Christ until He returns at the seventh trumpet.

Does God's Word Teach "Rapture"?

What we did not learn is anything of a rapture.

RAPTURE - A seizing and carrying away. Transport. Ecstasy. Extreme delight.

RESURRECTION - Restoring to life. Raising from the dead.

We did not learn anything of a rapture at least in the sense of being seized and carried away to heaven. One could say that when we are gathered back to Christ, since He is coming to Mount Zion, that we may be transported to be with Him there. Or, we are sure that every Christian would agree that Christ's return will be an extremely delightful occasion. Unfortunately though, when the word rapture is used it is not thought of to mean these things. It is thought to mean a seizing and a carrying away to heaven.

If we instead use the terms that are found in God's Word, such as, "gathering back to Christ" and "resurrection or raised" it would eliminate the confusion brought about by using the term "rapture".

The Word makes it clear that we do not gather back to Christ until His Second Coming which is at the last trumpet and at that time we will be raised to our spiritual bodies. Knowing the order of events, as is clearly stated in God's Word, gives a person an opportunity to prepare both physically and spiritually for the end-times.

As it is now, the rapture theory divides the body of Christ. Although a person might not decide to attend, or not attend, a particular church based on their beliefs regarding the rapture alone, it could and probably is in many instances a consideration.

Using the term "rapture" is also confusing in the sense that some believe in a pre-trib rapture, some mid-trib and others post-trib. It stands to reason without even opening God's Word, that all of these views regarding timing cannot be correct. But, once we do open God's Word we find not only that God is not the author of confusion, we in fact, find no evidence of a rapture at all. So, where did it come from and why?

The Rapture Theory?

The rapture theory in general, and specifically pre-trib, originated around the year 1830. Mid-trib and post-trib beliefs have since been derived from that beginning.

The Church (Christians), through the first 1,800 years of it's existence believed that they would not be gathered back to Christ until His Second Coming which they knew to be after the tribulation of the last days. Further, they had no expectations of being physically removed from the tribulation of the last days (if they happened to be the generation that would experience that tribulation) or any other tribulations, troubles or afflictions that they may have had to go through.

They were told to look forward to the "Blessed Hope" which they knew to be the actual, physical return of Jesus Christ to this earth, not a rapture.

So why then are we taught of a rapture today?

Set-Up for Deception

Satan wants to be God. He wants you to worship him. Naturally, a Christian is not going to do that knowingly. Therefore, Satan's main weapon through the tribulation of the last days will be deception. Jesus Himself warned us of this deception many times. What does this have to do with the rapture?

If you believe in a rapture, especially pre-trib or mid-trib then you essentially believe that Christ is going to appear before the anti-christ, to carry you away to heaven before the trouble begins. We find no evidence to substantiate this belief in God's Word. To the contrary, we can see quite clearly that the anti-christ is to appear first.

If Satan can con you into believing in the rapture, it will be one of his greatest successes in manipulating mankind into doubting the Word of God. How is that?

If you are being taught of a rapture, again especially pre-trib or mid-trib, that teaching likely encompasses the following message whether stated directly or by implication.

You will not experience the tribulation, you will not know who the anti-christ is, you do not need to concern yourself with prophecy regarding the last days, and therefore are exempt from the responsibility of watching the signs of the last days and thus being able to determine the season in which we live, as Christ admonished us repeatedly to do.

If this message is adhered to, one could be setting themselves up to worship the anti-christ (since he comes before Christ) because of their belief that Christ is coming first to rapture them away.

Although it is natural for us in the physical to avoid anything which would cause pain or discomfort, the physical aspect of hoping to be snatched away before the tribulation is quite insignificant in relation to the destiny of your soul. Worshiping Satan is not the way of obtaining eternal life.

Deception to Doubt

Also, if one were to adhere to this message and then "wake up" one day to find themselves in the middle of the period of tribulation, past the point in time that they had been taught the rapture was to occur, this could cause them to question the Word of God in general which in turn could lead to questioning their own salvation.

If you have been taught that Christ is going to rapture you away because you are a Christian and if you are then not raptured, does this mean you are not a Christian? (Questioning and doubt)

Satan's most effective tool used in coming against a Christian is doubt. Doubt means: distrust, uncertainty, disbelief and to question. We are told that without FAITH it is IMPOSSIBLE to please God. Faith means: confidence, trust, certainty and to believe. You can see that to have faith leaves no room for doubt. If Satan can cause you to doubt, questioning God's Word, then he has turned you away from having faith, which is unpleasing to our Father.

As we stated earlier, Satan wants to be God. He wants you to worship him. If you will not do that willingly, then he will attempt to obtain your worship through deception. At the very least he will attempt to take you away from Christ through doubt. The rapture theory could be most instrumental in helping Satan accomplish his goal.

We know that some would say that this is not at all in line with "what we have always heard." It was not in line with what we had always heard either. We would challenge you though, to refrain from using "what we have always heard" as a basis to adhere to the rapture theory.

What's the Question?

Why did Jesus and the apostles and the early Church not teach of a rapture? Why did the Church for 1,800 years believe that the final generation would go through the tribulation? Why did Jesus give us signs leading up to the end of the age? Why didn't he just say that the signs were irrelevant because we would not be on earth through that time? Why didn't Jesus just say He would carry us off to heaven before the tribulation?

Why hasn't God raptured other Christians throughout history off to heaven so they would not have to experience some of the tribulations and afflictions that they went through? Why did Jesus admonish us time and time again to watch the signs and be ready for His return? Why did Jesus warn us repeatedly about the deception in the last days? Why did Jesus warn us of false prophets and false teachings?

Why did the rapture theory not develop until the year 1830, fairly recent but yet long enough ago to develop a strong foothold and a large following in the Church today? Why all of the confusion regarding the timing of the "rapture"?

All of these questions, we believe, warrant consideration, even though the answer to some may be derived through speculation. The most important question to answer though is, what does God's Word say concerning the rapture? The answer to this question is the most important. It is of even greater significance if we are presently living in the end-times as many believe. We may very well be the generation to experience the tribulation of the last days and witness Christ's return.

It is not enough to base our belief of the rapture on "what we have always heard." Read and study God's Word and find out for yourself concerning the rapture: Is it written?

Scripture Index

Scripture Index   (Continued)

Judges 4:14-16,24,
chapter 5 Judges Debra song